Arduino

2020 Step-by-Step Guide for Absolute Beginners. Everything you need to know about Arduino.

Arduino

Copyright © 2020

All rights reserved.

ISBN: 9798616423146

CONTENTS

Introduction 5

Everything you need to know before starting with Arduino 8

Chapter 1: Step one: how to get started with Arduino. 15

Chapter 2: Step two: Install the Software 26

Install Arduino on Windows 26

Install Arduino on macOS 27

Install Arduino on Linux 28

Chapter 3: Step Three: Set up the Software 30

Windows 32

MacOS 33

Linux 34

Chapter 4: Step four: Checking the interaction of the board and the computer 35

Troubleshooting: It doesn't working 36

Light an LED! 37

Chapter 5: Step five: Introducing into the Arduino IDE 40

Chapter 6: Libraries 47

Chapter 7: Troubleshooting 52

External hardware 55

Debug 66

Chapter 8: Examples of simple projects for beginners based on Arduino 69

GSM alarm 69

LED cube 70

Wireless internet radio 72

Remote-controlled lawnmower 76

Conclusion 80

Introduction

Arduino is a small board containing an 8-bit or 32-bit microcontroller, as well as several other components. The latest generation models, such as Uno, are equipped with a USB interface and a number of pins for analog input and digital input and output.

The story of Arduino originates from the Institute for the Design of Interactions of the Italian city of Ivrea. This educational institution focuses on interacting with digital devices and systems.

The essence of the Arduino development concept is to simplify the creation of interactive objects or environments and the ability to make them more accessible. For this purpose, it was designed to be inexpensive and affordable, thus providing amateur developers, students and professionals the opportunity to create devices and projects that interact with the environment using sensors and actuators.

Standard examples of Arduino projects include simple robots, security systems, and motion sensors. There are many such examples.

Arduino is much more than just hardware. The microcontroller must be programmed. To do this, you will use the integrated development environment (IDE), which runs on personal computers. With it, users write programs known as sketches, using the C or C programming language.

Arduino is the modern equivalent of obsolete electronics kits from the recent past that were available from companies like Radio Shack and Heath.

The Arduino microcontroller comes with a bootloader, which greatly simplifies downloading programs to the board's flash memory. For comparison: the products of competitors Arduino requires the use of an external programmer.

In accordance with the ideology of the Arduino project, the programming process is simplified as much as possible, and we can do this using a personal computer.

Arduino is an ideal tool for learning the basics of electronics in general, as well as programming.

Since all the connectors on the Arduino boards are of standard types, we can expand the functionality of the Arduino base set by using the integrated boards known as shields. Due to the design of the connectors, they can be placed on top of each other, which makes it possible to create large and complex projects.

A number of Arduino boards are available to users. These include Uno, Duemilanove, Diecimila and Mega. All of them are intended for use with specific types of projects and therefore come with different technical characteristics. The most popular of these boards is Uno. It can be used for a wide range of projects.

Everything you need to know before starting with Arduino

In 2005, the Ivrea Interaction Design

Institute in Italy started a project of creating an open-source platform to be used for building various electronic projects, known as Arduino. The platform eventually gained worldwide popularity due to its accessibility and beginner-friendly features. Over the years since its inception, Arduino has garnered the attention and enthusiasm of hobbyists, artists, programmers, students and even hackers from all levels of experience. Being an open-source platform, it continues to grow with contributions from a diverse community of users that keep pushing the limits of its capabilities. In fact, Arduino has been the backbone behind thousands of projects and applications, from everyday objects to complex scientific equipment.

The Arduino platform consists of two components:

1. The hardware – A physical programmable circuit board, also known as the microcontroller. There are different types of Arduino boards.

2. The Software – The Integrated Development Environment (IDE) that runs on the computer, used for writing and uploading programming codes to the physical board.

Why Go Arduino?

Practically anyone can use Arduino. Experts are sure to have fun with building projects and sharing ideas with other users at online communities. For those with no experience with circuits and micro-controller programming, the platform is excellent for learning and experimenting. However, it is recommended that before exploring the wonders of Arduino, you should at least have a firm understanding of these fundamental concepts:

- The basics of electricity and circuitry
- Voltage, current, resistance and Ohm's law
- Polarity
- Integrated circuits (ICs)

- Digital logic
- Analog versus Digital
- Basic computer programming.

What makes Arduino a favorite among amateurs and experts alike is that, compared to other platforms and systems, it simplifies the process of working with microcontrollers. For a start, loading new codes to the board can simply be done with a USB cable, unlike previous programmable circuit boards where a separate piece of hardware has to be used. It is also a plus point that Arduino boards are relatively inexpensive compared to other micro-controller platforms, with some pre-assembled modules costing less than $50.

If those perks are not enough, here are some more reasons why Arduino is the platform to go for:

- Cross-platform – Arduino's IDE runs on Windows, Macintosh OSX, and Linux operating systems, whereas most micro-

controller systems are only compatible with Windows.
- Simple programming environment – The Arduino IDE uses a simplified version of C++, making it easier for beginner to learn how to program, yet flexible enough for advance users to get creative and ambitious with.
- Open source and extensible hardware – Arduino board plans are published under a Creative Common license, allowing circuit designers to create their own version of the module, extending it and improving upon it.
- Open source and extensible software – The Arduino IDE is published as open source tools that experienced programmers can expand on, through C++ libraries. You can also learn the AVR-C programming language from Arduino, just as you can also add AVR-C code directly into Arduino programs.
- Backed by a supportive community – If you are absolutely new to the platform and don't know where to begin, there is

a wealth of information to be found online due to the popularity of Arduino. You will never run out of resources to learn from, and you can even find pre-coded projects to work on right away.

What can Arduino do for You?

Arduino was designed with the creative and innovative in mind, regardless of experience level. Artists, designers, electricians, engineers, programmers and science enthusiasts can use it to create interactive objects and environments. Among the things Arduino can interact with include motors, speakers, LEDs, GPS units, cameras, TVs, smart-phones and even the internet. With Arduino, one can build low cost scientific instruments, do programming for robotics, build interactive prototypes of architectural designs and create installations for musical instruments to experiment with sound, build new video game hardware – and this is just the tip of the iceberg! So, whether your project entails building a robot, a heating blanket, a festive lighting display or a fortune-telling machine, Arduino can serve as a base for your electronic projects.

Chapter 1: Step one: how to get started with Arduino.

As the Arduino platform is ever expanding, continuous learning is necessary as there is always something new to discover. You will be introduced to the basic Arduino components, what you will need and how to set them up. Obviously, you are going to need the two essentials: an Arduino board and the software installed (available free for download on the official Arduino website).

Arduino Board

Before you start shopping around for hardware, you need to know some basics about Arduino boards and their features. There are several types of Arduino boards available for purchase, each with different capabilities. Although they may differ in look and capabilities, you will find most boards have the majority of these components in common:

1. USB and Barrel Jack – Every board will have a means for it to be connected to a power source. Almost all Arduino boards come with USB connection, since this is how you will be uploading codes onto them. You can also connect to a wall power supply via the barrel jack.

2. Pins – The boards' pins are where you construct circuits by connecting wires. There are several types of pins on Arduino boards, each meant for a specific functions. Here is what you will normally find: • GND: Short for Ground, these pins are used to ground your

circuit.

- 5V and 3.3V: These pins supply 5 Volts and 3.3 Volts of power, respectively.
- Analog: You can identify this row of pins under the 'Analog In' label. They are used for reading signals from analog sensors, and convert those signals into digital values.
- Digital: Across from the analog pins, under the 'Digital' label, are the pins to be used for digital input and output. For example, telling when a button is pressed (input), so that an LED lights up (output). • PWM: In a lot of Arduino boards, there is the label (PWM~) next to 'Digital'. It means that the pins can be used as normal digital pins, and also for a type of signal called Pulse-Width Modulation
- AREF: A short form for Analog Reference, this is the pin which can be used to set an external voltage as the upper limit for the analog pins (between 0 and 5 Volts), although it is mostly left alone.

3. Reset button – This button is self-

explanatory; pushing it will connect the rest pin to ground, and restart any code loaded onto the board. This is useful for testing your programmed codes multiple times. It does not, however, functions to reset everything to a clean slate and wipe away any problems.

4. Power LED Indicator – This is a tiny LED that can be identified with the word 'ON' next to it. It will light up when you plug the board into a power source, and if it doesn't, it means you have to re-check your circuit because something is wrong.

5. Transmit (TX) and Receive (RX) LEDs – Not to be confused with the TX and RX markings by the 0 and 1 digital pins, the LEDs with these markings will give you a visual indication whenever the board is transmitting or receiving data, such as when you load a new program onto the board.

6. Main Integrated Circuit (IC) – This is the black piece with metal legs that is attached to every board. It is basically the brains of an Arduino board. The main IC differs from board to board, though most are from the ATmega line of IC's by the ATMEL company.

It is important to know the IC and board type before loading up a new program from the Arduino IDE. You can usually find this information written on the top side of the IC.

7. Voltage regulator – As its name implies, this component controls the amount of voltage that is allowed into the Arduino board. It functions by turning away extra voltage let into the board. But it has its limits though; it cannot handle anything over 20 Volts. So, a word of caution: DO NOT use a power supply greater than 20 Volts! It will overpower and destroy your Arduino. The recommended voltage for most models is 6 to 12 Volts.

Arduino Family

The Arduino board has gone through considerable changes since it was first introduced, in order to meet the various demands and challenges of its users. More than just the 8-bit boards, Arduino have boards built for various applications, from Internet of Things (IoT) applications to wearable items. All of them are, of course, open-source, which further empowers users to build derivatives and customize them to fit specific needs. The following are a few options that are considered most suitable for the Arduino novice:

- Arduino UNO (R3) – The UNO is often considered to be the definitive Arduino board. It is well-equipped with everything you need to get started, with 14c digital input/output pins – six of which can be used as Pulse Width Modulation (PWM) outputs – six analog inputs, a USB connection, a power jack and many more. Simply connect it to any power source, whether it is a computer with a USB cable, an AC-to-DC adapter or battery, and you are good to get started. Regardless of your Arduino expertise, you can never go wrong with the UNO.
- Arduino Mega (2560) – The Mega board is a few notches above the UNO; kind of like its big brother. It has an impressive

54 digital input/output pins, of which 14 can be used as PWM outputs, 16 analog inputs, plus everything else you can find on the UNO and also functions the same way. If you have a project that requires a lot of digital input/outputs, such as for a lot of LED lights or buttons, the Mega may be the board for the job.
- Arduino Leonardo – The Leonardo board offers a cheaper and simpler alternative, as it is the first Arduino development board to use one microcontroller with built-in USB. Because of its direct USB handling, code libraries are available that allows the board to emulate a computer keyboard, mouse and much more.
- Arduino Mega ADK – This board is basically a specialized version of the Arduino Mega board. It is specifically designed for interfacing with Android smartphones.
- LilyPad Arduino – Thinking about making a cat-suit that lights up? The LilyPad is the wearable e-textile board

you need. Designed by Leah Buechley, engineer and co-author of the book, Sew Electric, the innovative board was created with a large connecting pad and flat back that allows it to be sewn into clothing with conductive thread. And it is even washable!

- Arduino NG, Diecimila and duemilanove – Collectively known as Legacy Versions of the UNO, these boards are basically the granddaddies of the Arduino. The legacy boards lack some key features of other newer boards. For instance, the Diecimila and NG have a jumper next to the USB port and require manual selection of either USB or battery power. The NG also requires holding down the Reset button for a few seconds before uploading a program. It should be noted, however, the legacy boards are still being tinkered and improved upon by Arduino enthusiasts. They are worth looking into once you gain more knowledge and experience with Arduino.

Genuino. What is it?

If you are shopping for Arduino boards outside of America, you may find Genuino boards that look identical. Don't worry; you are not being duped by an imitation product! Genuino is Arduino's sister-brand, created by the same team, and used for boards and products sold outside of the US. The Genuino brand certifies the authenticity of boards and products to be in line with Arduino's philosophy of open-source hardware. The brand has alliances with market-leading manufacturers in Asia, Europe, South America, Canada and Africa, making the Arduino hardware available worldwide. You can think of Genuino boards as the identical twins of Arduino boards that live in foreign countries. All Genuino boards have the similar quality, components and characteristics as their Arduino counterpart. So, depending on which part of the world you live, you may find a

Genuino UNO board when looking to buy an Arduino UNO. That's just fine; you're still getting the real deal. It should be noted though, that not all Arduino boards – especially lesser known ones – have a Genuino twin.

Other You could Use

An Arduino board cannot do much on its own, so you will need to hook it up with something. There are plenty of hardware options one can fix onto their Arduino boards that will be overwhelming for the beginner to learn. Hence, we will only be introducing you to two handy items that are easy to hook onto an Arduino boards and bringing your projects to life – sensors and shields. There is a lot of fun to be had with sensors. Hook one up to your Arduino board, and add some simple programming code, you can then make your board sense and measure practically anything – light, temperature, physical pressure, distance proximity, barometric pressure and radioactivity. You can also build devices to scan fingerprint, detect motions of animals or people, and signals from remote controls. Additionally, you can do even more with shields, which are pre-built circuit boards that can fit on top of your Arduino boards. With shields, you can program your Arduino to connect to the internet, control LCD screens, control motors and provide cellular communication and lots of other cool stuff, limited only by your knowledge and imagination!

Chapter 2: Step two: Install the Software

In this chapter, we will briefly look at installing Arduino on the most common operating systems. Depending on your operating system, you may choose the right type of installation of the software.

Install Arduino on Windows

The software is not bundled with Arduino. You need to download it to your computer from the Arduino website. This is a Windows 10 system, but the same instructions apply to Windows 8 and others. In order to install the software, you need to go to arduino.cc/en/main/software.

Download the Arduino IDE

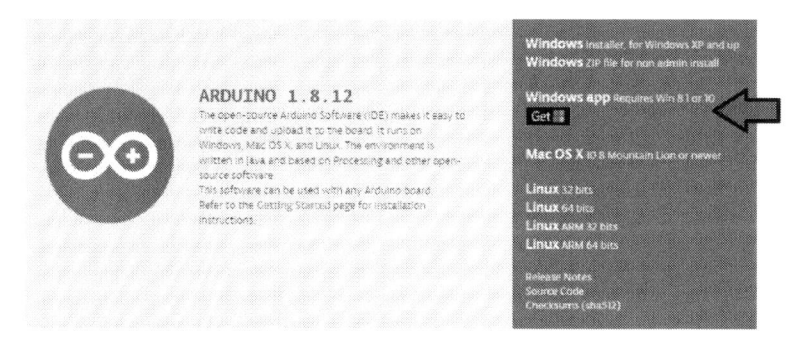

Install Arduino on macOS

The first thing to do is go to arduino.cc/en/main/software. Under the Arduino 1.0.5 heading, click the macOS link to start the download. When finished, go to the download folder, where you see the Arduino icon.

Attention! The described instructions demonstrate the installation of Arduino in OS X 10.8 Mountain Lion. Installation may vary depending on the version of your operating system.

You need, Drag the Arduino icon to the Applications folder. In addition, you can drag it to the Dock, from where you can easily access the application. The Dock panel allows you to place icons of frequently used applications for easy launch.

Click the Arduino icon to open the program. You will see a notification that Arduino is a program downloaded from the Internet, and a request specifying whether you really want to open it. There is no threat to open it, so click the Open button.

After that, the Arduino IDE interface will open. Now you can start writing code to program the microcontroller.

Install Arduino on Linux

Installing Arduino on a Linux operating system requires a slightly different approach than on Windows and macOS. There are many different versions of Linux, we took the most common version of the operating system and describe the installation using its example. The installation process may vary slightly depending on the version. And so, install it on Ubuntu, one of the most popular alternative operating systems. On the Ubuntu desktop, click on the Ubuntu Software Center icon. When the application center opens, enter Arduino in the search field in the upper right part of the window. The search program will automatically detect the correct version of Arduino. When you see it in the list of search results, click on the corresponding item to display the Installation button in the right part of the window. Confirm the above action by entering your password in Ubuntu in the next window, and then click the Authenticate button. The Arduino icon appears on the sidebar of the Linux operating system. Click on it to open the Arduino IDE.

Chapter 3: Step Three: Set up the Software

You have an Arduino board and the software; it is time to get down to business! In the sections that follow, you will be guided in a step-by-step process to do a few things. However, the instructions can be applied, with minor modifications, to any Arduino board of your choice.

Here are the four pieces of equipment you

will need to begin your Arduino journey:
- A computer that runs on Windows (XP or above), Mac, or Linux operating the system, with the Arduino IDE installed
- An Arduino micro-controller (a.k.a. the circuit board)
- A USB A-to-B cable for connecting your Arduino board to the computer, or one that fits your board of choice (be aware that some boards will require an A-to-Mini-B cable)
- An LED

But first, we will set up our Arduino.

Arduino setup

In essence, Arduino setup boils down to connecting the board to a computer and then installing drivers. This may cause problems, but, as a rule, this happens with computers running outdated operating systems. The Arduino board will work with almost any operating system. But the older the system, the harder it will be to configure the Arduino. The first step that you need to do is to connect the board to the computer using the USB cable, which can be found in the kit. Once you have done this, the green LED on the board should light up to indicate that the board is receiving power. What happens afterward depends on your operating system.

Windows

Recent Windows operating systems work well with Arduino. If you work with Windows 8 or 10, the setup will work without problems. Connect the board to the computer, and after a while, the Device Setup window will appear. Please note that in this example we are setting up Arduino on the Windows 8 operating system.

Attention! On computers running the Windows operating system, Arduino will always use the COM3 port.

The Windows 8/10 operating system will automatically detect and install the Arduino driver - you do not have to take any action. Installation takes only a few minutes, and then the window closes. To check if the driver is installed correctly, go to the Device manager component of the Control Panel window. Click the triangle in the Ports line and you should see that the Arduino is configured to use the COM3 port.

MacOS

The Arduino setup procedure for macOS Lion, Mountain Lion, Leopard, and Snow Leopard (and later) is a straightforward process and should be straightforward. Earlier versions may cause problems.
You just need to, Connect the board to the computer using the USB cable. A dialog box will open.
Next, click the Network Preferences button and the Apply button in the next window. If you look on the left side of this window, then (most likely) you will see that the Arduino item is displayed with the "Not configured"

label. Do not pay attention to this, the Arduino software is correctly configured and ready to use. The message "Not configured" is erroneous - ignore it.

Linux

When using a modern Linux operating system such as Ubuntu 14.04 and later, the Arduino board does not require any configuration. Just plug in the board using the USB cable, launch the Arduino software, and you can get started.

Attention! Earlier versions may cause problems. We recommend that you consult one of the many websites dedicated to such issues. This can be done at playground.arduino.ee/learning/linux.

Chapter 4: Step four: Checking the interaction of the board and the computer

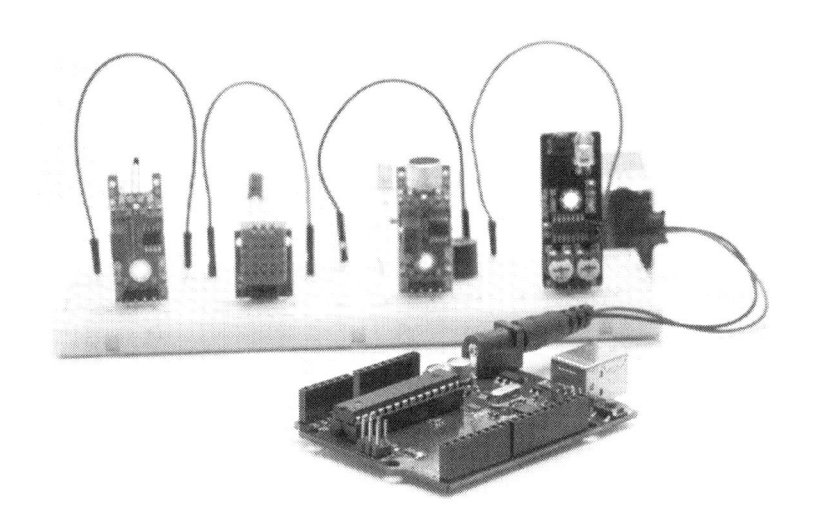

After setting up the Arduino, before moving on, you need to check whether the Arduino board is actually communicating with the computer. Do it as follows:

1. Connect the board to the computer using the USB cable.
2. Launch the Arduino IDE software on your

computer. (From the File - »Examples menu, select Basics
Blink.) So you load the Blink sketch into the code editing window.
3. Click the Upload icon in the upper left corner.
4. You will see the following: firstly, a message stating that the download has completed is displayed in the lower left of the screen. And secondly, the LED indicator of pin 13 on the board will turn on and off. All this suggests that the board and the computer are exchanging data.

Troubleshooting: It doesn't working

If you followed all the steps above, but you can't upload the sketch to your Arduino for it to launch, it could be due to problems with one of the processes. Try running through these troubleshooting measures:
1. Make sure you select the right board under the Tools > Board menu. In case you choose to use another board besides the UNO (as in

the example), check the IC on the board. For instance, newer Arduino Duemilanove boards come with an ATmega328, while older ones have an ATmega168. So, make sure you select the right option.
2. Check that the proper port is selected in the Tools > Serial Port menu.
3. Check to see if the drivers for your board are properly installed in the Tools > Serial Port menu in the Arduino IDE, with your board connected. There should be an additional item that wasn't there when your board is not plugged in.

Light an LED!

Having successfully activated your Arduino, let's try doing a little bit more with it. The following is a common learning project suitable for complete beginners in circuitry. For this task, you will need an LED and your Arduino that has already been launched (following the previous instructions).
1. Plug in your board.

2. Open another example sketch: File > Examples > Basics > BareMinimum. This will open a new window with a simple sketch that acts as the framework for your program.

3. Connect the LED's anode (the longer pin) to pin 13 on the Arduino board, and the cathode (the shorter pin) to the adjacent GND pin.

4. Under the setup() section of the sketch, add the code: pin Mode(13, OUTPUT);. This is the command that will run once to configure the board and get it ready to do as you program.

5. Add the following under the loop() section: digital Write(13, HIGH);. This sets the pin 13 as an output pin with high voltage level (5 Volt).When complete; your sketch should look like this:

```
void setup(){
pinMode(13, OUTPUT);
}
void loop(){
digitalWrite(13, HIGH);
}
```

Hit the Upload button and wait for the Done

Uploading message to show in the status bar.
The LED should light up.

Chapter 5: Step five: Introducing into the Arduino IDE

Arduino Development Environment

Your computer is now equipped with the Arduino Integrated Development Environment (IDE), which is configured to communicate with the Arduino board. Using the environment, you can write code to program the microcontroller. In Arduino, these programs are called sketches.

Important! Uploading the sketch to the microcontroller on the Arduino board and observing possible changes in the board's behavior will demonstrate that everything is working properly. In essence, the Arduino IDE interface is similar to a word processor. It has four main sections: a menu bar, a toolbar, a text editor, and a status area. The Arduino IDE is written in Java and is based on open-source software such as Processing, avr-GCC, etc. Sketches are called that way because they are based on the Processing programming language, which allows users to create programs as fast as if they were writing an idea into a notebook — a sketchbook.

Title bar

At the top there is a title bar that displays the name of the current sketch and the IDE version (Arduino 1.0.5-r2).

Menu bar

Below the title bar is a menu bar. It contains the following menus:

1. File menu

The File menu contains a number of commands, from universal ones - New, Open, Close, etc. - to commands unique to Arduino. The latter include:
• Sketchbook - this command displays a list of all the sketches you created and provides an easy way to open them;
• Examples - here you can access a large number of pre-written sketches. Since they are written using open source code and are free, you can freely modify them for your own purposes.

2. "Edit" menu

Many of the commands on the Edit menu will be familiar to you. Some that you may not

know include:
• Copy for Forum - this command copies the code of your sketch to the clipboard in a format compatible with the Arduino forum;
• Copy as HTML, which allows you to copy the sketch code to the clipboard in HTML format, suitable for placement on a web page;
• Comment / Uncomment — commented blocks of text are not loaded onto the Arduino board. Typically, comments are used to remind important details or explain how a sketch works.

3. The Sketch menu

The Sketch menu consists of several options that help you manage your sketches:
• Verify / Comply - this command checks the code you wrote for errors and then "compiles" it into a format, understandable to the microcontroller;
• Upload - selecting this command, you will upload the code from a text editor to the Arduino board;
• Upload Using Programmer - this command

allows you to upload sketches using an external system programmer (ISP); but this is for advanced users, not for beginners. There are several reasons why you will want to use an external programmer: faster boot time, lack of serial connection and the increase in memory available to your sketch.
• Import library allows you to add a sketch library;
• Add File adds the file to the sketch, which appears in a new tab in the sketch window.
Arduino's software automatically saves each sketch you write to the sketch folder. The Show Sketch Folder command opens a folder containing the current sketch.

Tools menu

The Tools' menu provides various commands that may be useful when working with Arduino:
• Auto Format performs auto-formatting of the sketch code to make it easier to read;
• Fix Encoding & Reload - fix encoding errors that may have a negative effect on the sketch;

- Board - allows you to select your board from the list of Arduino boards;
- Serial Monitor - displays serial data and is useful for debugging.

Toolbar

The toolbar contains icons of the most frequently used commands so that you do not need to spend time searching for them. They are: Verify, Upload, New, Open and Save.

The Increase Indent and Decrease Indent menu items are essentially formatting commands that allow you to create your sketches in such a way that their code is easier to read.

String and Status Area

The status bar displays messages about the status of current operations. It also serves as an indicator of progress so you can see how the download is done. The status area is used to display error messages.

Text editor

Here you enter the code when writing sketches. The work of the editor is much like the work of a word processor. Right-clicking on the text will open the editing menu, which offers standard editing commands such as Cut, Sora, Paste, etc.

Chapter 6: Libraries

In fact, the Arduino library is a modified sketch that can be easily shared with other users, as well as to simplify code updates.
Libraries allow you to quickly add features to a sketch, thus increasing its functionality. For example, you can program your Arduino board to use a specific type of equipment. Instead of writing the necessary code yourself, you can simply import it into your

sketch as an existing sketch.

There are many reasons to create libraries. These include simplifying use, organizing code, increasing code readability, and logical decentralization.

Arduino's software may already contain the required library; You can also download the desired sketch from the Internet. On the Internet, you will find documented code for a huge number of popular projects and functions of many Arduino users. You can also freely integrate such code into your sketches.

When you become an experienced programmer, you can write libraries yourself. Now we will look at some libraries that come with the Arduino Uno board.

You will find them by selecting the menu command Sketch Import Library in the Arduino window. Available libraries cover the most popular categories of Arduino projects, and you are sure to find something here that will be useful in one of your own projects.

• EEPROM is an abbreviation for "Electrically Programmable Read-Only Memory Device".

This type of non-volatile memory is used in computers and other electronic devices to store small amounts of data that must be saved when the power is turned off. The library allows you to write and read from the EEPROM component on the Arduino board.

• Ethernet — you will use this library when connecting the Ethernet shield to the Arduino board. It allows the shield to connect to the Internet as either a server or a client.

• Liquid Crystal - This library allows the Arduino board to control liquid crystal displays (LCDs). The library is based on the Hitachi HD44780 chipset (or compatible equivalent), which is found in most text displays.

Most of the Arduino libraries you can find on the Internet are open source. This means that you can use them in your own projects.

• GSM - The Global System for Mobile Communications (GSM) is an international cellular communications service that is available in Europe and other parts of the world. This library allows the Arduino board to perform most of the operations that you can do using a phone with a GSM module: make and receive voice calls, send and receive SMS messages, and connect to the Internet via GPRS protocol.

SD - this library is used with shields that allow you to connect an SD memory card. These memory cards are widely used in portable devices such as smartphones, digital cameras, GPS navigators, etc. The SD library allows both writing and reading from SD cards and supports the FAT16 and FAT32 file systems.

Wi-Fi — When used with the Arduino Wi-Fi shield, this library allows the Arduino board to connect to the Internet. It can function either as a server, accepting incoming connections, or as a client, making outgoing connections. The library supports WEP and WPA2 Personal encryption, but not WPA2 Enterprise.

Data Protection Protocols (WEP) and Wi-Fi Protected Access II (WPA2) protect networks by encrypting transmitted data.

Stepper - This library allows you to control unipolar and bipolar stepper motors with the

Arduino board. To use this library, you need a stepper motor with hardware to control it.

Servo - This library is used in conjunction with amateur servos. These are electric motors that have built-in mechanisms and a shaft, as well as precise control. The Servo Library supports up to 12 motors on most Arduino boards and up to 48 on Arduino Mega.

Firmata is a standard communication protocol that allows you to control the Arduino board using software on your computer. The Firmata library can also be used to selectively send and receive data between an Arduino device and software running on your computer.

SPI - Serial Peripheral Interface (SPI) is an interface bus commonly used to send data between microcontrollers and small peripherals such as shift registers, sensors, and SD cards. When it comes to SPI connection, there is always a master device that controls peripheral devices. The SPI library allows you to communicate with SPI devices using the Arduino board as a master.

Chapter 7: Troubleshooting

Experienced Arduino users know that potential problems will not belong in coming. The more complex the project, the higher the likelihood of difficulties. Of course, beginners will have difficulty working even with simple projects.

It doesn't matter what experience you have with the Arduino board, problems can also arise due to a number of different skills needed for many projects - electronics, programming, computer technology, mechanics, carpentry, metalworking, etc. All this combined adds even more problems and difficulties.

Obviously, the more you understand what exactly you are doing and how the various components of the project interact with each other, the more likely it is that you will be able to fix problems as they arise. Thus, knowledge is the most important weapon in your arsenal. Learn as much as possible, in particular from the fields of electronics, computer engineering, and programming. Not having good knowledge in these areas, when working with Arduino you will encounter great difficulties.

Hardware

The malfunctions in your projects can be related to either software or hardware. You can check hardware issues as described below.

Depending on the nature of the problem, you can first make sure that your Arduino board is working and is properly connected to your computer.

Faulty or faulty cable connections often cause hardware problems. Always check these connections first.

Work out the following list.

- ✓ Make sure your computer is on (you'll be surprised how many people neglect this most basic step).
- ✓ Connect Arduino to your computer with a USB cable.
- ✓ Check the PWR on the board. It should burn with a soft green light. If so, he indicates that the Arduino board is connected to the computer and is powered.
- ✓ If the PWR is off or dim, first check to see if the USB cable is securely connected to the Arduino board and to the computer. Then try connecting the

cable to another USB port, this option often helps. Finally, try replacing the cable.
✓ If you're using an external power adapter rather than a computer for Arduino, make sure the adapter works properly. You can do this by connecting it to another device. Also make sure that the cable used is of good quality and that it is connected to the correct contacts on the Arduino board.

External hardware

External hardware includes chains connected to the Arduino board, sensors, electric motors, etc. If there is no power supply, very often the problem is simply a poor connection or lack thereof. Replacing faulty components is a great way to diagnose faults. Once you've eliminated power and connection sources, identify the problem by replacing the components where possible. In this way, sensors and electric motors can be checked.

Diagnosing faults on the circuit board requires special test equipment, such as a multimeter (and the ability to use it).

Installation problems

We've previously written how to set up an Arduino fee with a computer. You may have problems when you do this, which depends a lot on the operating system installed on your computer.

Windows

As a rule, it's not difficult for Windows users to set up Arduino. In particular, this is possible if you use Windows 8 or later this OS does it for you automatically.
Council. If you have a problem trying to connect the Arduino board with your computer, it's very common to be a non-performing driver.
If your computer runs Windows 7, Windows Vista, or Windows HR, you'll probably have problems. These operating systems may have

difficulty finding and installing the Arduino driver, which is manifested in the next error message (or similar).

The Windows Device Manager lets you control all your computer-connected hardware, including the Arduino fee. The solution in this situation is to install the driver manually. You can do it this way.

Open the Start menu and click on the Control Panel. Then open the Device Manager component. It lists all the equipment installed on your system, including the Arduino fee.

Twist the list down until you see the Arduino inscription; If you don't see this label, it may be under Ports. Next to it may be an exclamation point that warns that the fee has been set incorrectly.

Click the right button on the Arduino line and select Update Driver Software in the context menu. Then select Browse Moo Computer for Driver Software.

Click browse and go to the C:Program Files (x86) directory. Find a Arduino.int file here. Select it and click Next. The Windows operating system will install the driver.

Now there should be a connection between your Arduino board and your computer.

You can also type the word Arduino into the Windows search engine. You'll find it on the Start menu.

Mac OS

The Arduino customization process in macOS Snow Leopard, Leopard, Mountain Lion, Lion and later versions is a similar process and should not be difficult.

However, as with earlier versions of Windows and Linux operating systems, setting up Arduino in earlier versions of mac OS can cause problems.

Arduino's macOS software comes in a zip archive, and damage can occur when unpacked or unzipped. Sometimes you get an error message and you'll be aware of the kind of problem that has occurred. But often the message may be missing.

Either way, try unpacking the archive with another archive program. There are many such programs. A good example is the 7-zip and WinRAR programs.

Another possible problem might be an outdated version of Java on your computer. In this case, you should receive an error message; if that happens, just download the latest version of the program from the Java website.

If you receive a Link error message, the solution in this situation is to upgrade to the most up-to-date version of macOS. Early versions contain incompatible system libraries.

If you're considering using the Arduino board with the Linux operating system, the best you can recommend is to use the most up-to-date version. This will help you avoid the many problems that would arise with early versions.

Linux

As we mentioned, setting up Arduino in early versions of Linux operating systems can be a challenge, and there's not enough room to describe problem-solving in this book. At the same time, there are a number of online resources where you can find help, such as www.linux.org.

Syntax errors

The Arduino is a computer, although simple enough. Like all computers, he does not have the ability to think for himself, but only responds to the instructions that the user sets him. These instructions (sketch code) must be written so that the computer recognizes them. Otherwise, he will simply ignore them and take no action.

The rules that determine how to write code are called syntax, and you need to study them to program. Your Arduino board. If you do not, you cannot write a sketch that will be accepted by the Arduino validation process or compiler. The syntax is a term used to describe a set of rules for writing code.

The incorrect syntax is probably the most common mistake that beginners make, and it always leads to the same result - the verification process simply stops when an error is detected.

Fortunately, the compiler tells you exactly where the error is located, as well as the type of error that occurred. Consider the example below. Typical syntax errors include: missing a semicolon at the end of the instruction, lack of opening / closing brackets, and errors / typos in command names. The compiler found that the parentheses were missing at the end of the void setup function. This function should be of the form void setup (). The program highlighted the line and indicated in the panel at the bottom of the window that the parameter for the function from line 13 was not declared. The description of the error is often incomprehensible and may mean nothing to the beginner.

This is all the information you need to fix the error.

Port monitor

The port monitor is an Arduino development environment tool that allows you to communicate with the Arduino board through a serial port. With it, you can send and receive data.

The ability to send / receive data and, in particular, view the received data makes the port monitor a very useful debugging tool. With it, you can analyze the code for errors and quickly fix them.

Before you can use it, you need to connect your Arduino board to your computer using a USB cable. Then you need to open the Serial Monitor window. This can be done in three different ways.

The Serial Monitor window is used to debug Arduino sketches and to view data transmitted by working sketches.

Open the Arduino development environment and from the menu at the top select Tools -> Serial Monitor.

Click on the Serial Monitor tab in the toolbar.

In fact, the Serial Monitor window is a separate terminal.

On the keyboard, press Ctrl + Shift + M. Whichever method you choose, the Serial Monitor window shown below appears. The keyboard shortcut Ctrl + Shift + M provides a quick way to open the Serial Monitor window. If the Serial Monitor window does not appear, the problem may be that the Arduino is using the wrong port. Launch the Device Manager tool in the Windows operating system and click the triangle to the left of the Ports (COM & LPT) - Ports (COM & LPT) item. This will let you know which port the operating system assigned to your Arduino board. Return to the Arduino development environment and select the menu command Tools -> Serial Port. When you launch the Serial Monitor window, each sketch currently downloaded will automatically restart. Pay attention to this. Make sure that the port that is assigned to your Arduino board in the Device Manager window is selected. The Serial Monitor window should now open. Text is transferred to the Arduino board through the Serial Monitor window by entering text in the field at the top of the window and pressing the Send button. Please note that the Serial Monitor tool will not be able to send / receive data if you did not include the corresponding code in the sketch, that is, you did not tell the sketch that this should be done.

You must tell the Serial Monitor tool that you want to send / receive data by including the appropriate code in the sketch.

At the bottom of the Serial Monitor window, you will see three parameters.

Speed, bits / second - this is the speed with which the Serial Monitor tool receives and transfers data to the Arduino board. The default value is 9600 baud.

Line End Detection - This drop-down list provides you with four options with which you can set the end of the line label sent by the Serial Monitor tool. In addition to the Newline item, you can choose options: No line ending, Carriage return and Both NL & CR.

"Carriage Return" and "New Line" are ASCII characters that are sent by pressing the Enter key on the keyboard. "Carriage Return" indicates that the cursor will return to the beginning of the line, while "New Line" determines that the cursor will be moved to the beginning of a new line.

Auto scroll - check this box if you want the last lines to be always visible in the sketch. Otherwise, you will have to manually scroll through the code.

Although the Serial Monitor tool provided by the Arduino board is useful, there are equally convenient alternatives. These include:

When establishing a connection with Arduino, you are not limited to the Serial Monitor tool. There are a number of third-party programs that you can use.

Processing - a free application for the operating system Windows, macOS and Linux;

CoolTerm - a free application for the operating system Windows, macOS and Linux;

puTTY is an open-source application for the

Windows and Linux operating systems; CuteCom is an open-source application that runs on the Linux operating system.

Debug

Before you use the Serial Monitor tool to fix a skit malfunction, or to debug (as the process is called), you should use it and let you know what you expect it to do. This means adding two pieces of code to the sketch that needs to be analyzed.

The first piece of code uses a port monitor and looks like this:

Serial.begin

Serial.begin is one of the many features available in The Serial's built-in library in Arduino. In brackets, you need to enter the desired speed of data (information). A 9600 is a standard value of approximately 1,000 characters per second. The code will look like this:

Serial .begin (9600);

Your sketch should trigger Serial .begin

before it can use the port monitor. This code is usually placed inside the setup function.

Whatever speed you put in brackets, make sure the same speed is chosen in the Serial Monitor window - if the speeds are different, you'll only see an incomprehensible set of characters in the Serial Monitor window.

The second piece of code is important from the point of view of debugging. It has the following look:

Seria 1. print In

If the data speed you choose doesn't match the value in your sketch code, the characters in the Serial Monitor window will be unreadable.

Function Serial. printin tells the port monitor that you need to display the text in the Serial Monitor window without it, the Serial Monitor window will open, but will remain empty.

If you specify instructions in brackets, such as the output of the sensor, Serial.println will display this value in the Serial Monitor window. This will allow you to immediately see if the value is correct. If you don't see the value, you'll know there's a problem, as well as its approximate location.

To debug, you can use Serial.printin as follows: if you have no idea which piece of code the problem is in, you can simply put a lot of copies of The Serial.println throughout the sketch code, and Then, when the sketch is launched, just watch the Serial Monitor window.

If you suspect an error in a particular section or line of code, you can fix a more selective malfunction.

The Serial Library in Arduino contains a number of features that can help you debug the code.

Chapter 8: Examples of simple projects for beginners based on Arduino

GSM alarm

The goal of this project is to create a security alarm with a large radius of action that can be used at home (or elsewhere for the same purpose).
It consists of an Arduino Uno board, a standard GSM / GPRS modem based on the

SIM900A chipset, and an intrusion detector (for example, an infrared proximity sensor or light sensor). The system is powered by a 12 V DC power supply or battery.

When the system is triggered by an attempted entry, an SMS message is sent to the mobile phone number indicated in the code. The system is also equipped with an "alarm call" function, which initiates a phone call when activated. Using it, a "missed call" warning is generated.

LED cube

Built of 512 LED lights, as well as a large number of integrated circuits with a shear register, resistors, transistors, capacitors and many meters of wires, the LED cube, however, serves no useful purpose.

However, this is an interesting object, offering almost unlimited number of light combinations, which will be quite entertaining - children, for example, will like a light show, which can be arranged with its help.

The LED cube consists of eight layers of LED lights, located at an equal distance and connected by a wire with a diameter of 0.22 mm. Thanks to the space between the LED lights, we can see them all on eight layers at a time, which gives the cube a three-dimensional effect. ☐

If you decide to assemble this device, remember that you will need hundreds of LED lights. They can be bought online at very low prices. However, the quality of such diodes can be quite mediocre. If you do not want to constantly replace faulty LED lights, we advise you to purchase only quality components.

This is a classic Arduino board project that requires a number of different skills. Not only do you need to know how to program the Arduino fee, you also need to understand how to design and create electrical circuits.

In addition, each layer should be the same as the previous one, and this requires a very accurate assembly.

The practical side of this project, i.e. creating

and stacking layers in a rigid design, is quite complex. When creating a cube of much smaller sizes, 2x2x2 is first recommended to do all the necessary calculations.

Wireless internet radio

The Skube project, developed at the Copenhagen Institute of Interactive Design, is part of a larger module to create a permeable user interface. It demonstrates how useful Arduino can be for prototyping and development.

For a note. Skube is a portable wireless internet radio. It can be connected to the user's Last.fm account and download music, as well as use the Spotify platform to search for and play audio recordings.

The motivation for developing the Skube device was the realization that with the development of the trend of listening to digital music on the Internet, modern portable music players are not adapted for this environment and therefore unsuitable.

Add to this the fact that the procedure of exchanging music in public places is neither convenient nor simple. Especially when people have such different musical preferences.

The result is a music player that allows you to interact with digital music services such as Spotify without the need for computer devices. All features can be controlled directly from the Skube device.

When one Skube connects to another, their playlists are shuffled. If you like the composition recorded in your friend's Skube memory, just click the heart-shaped button to add music to your playlist.

Each Skube device provides two modes, Playlist and Lawsuit. We can choose one of the modes simply by touching the top of Skube. Playlist mode plays songs with Skube, and Search mode searches for songs similar to those already recorded in Skube's memory. The device easily helps to find new music that you will have to taste.

When two Skube devices are connected to each other, they work as a single player, in which all the tracks from the playlists are mixed. This allows you to control multiple Skube from a single device.

The interface is designed to be intuitive and easy to use. By flipping Skube, you'll change the modes, the touch will cause playback, or skip the composition, and if you flip Skube to the front side, the device will be turned off.

The heart of the system is the Arduino board, installed in all Skube devices. Also inside is the Hiye module, which provides wireless communications to the devices. It allows Skube devices to share data with each other.

Skube contains a number of sensors that respond to the various actions by which the user controls the device (e.g., easy tapping on the surface of the device, flip, etc.). The input from these sensors is sent to Arduino, interpreting them and sending the necessary commands to the rest of the system.

These devices also contain Shield FM radio. The purpose of this module is to play music.

Hiye wireless modules, which were mentioned earlier, are also used to connect and control Skube using a computer.

Hie's wireless modules use the IEEE802.15.4 network protocol for a fast dot-group or dot-to-point connection.

This can be done using a visual programming language called Mach, which has been specifically designed for music and multimedia.

Two well-known music services, Spotify and Last.fm, provide special application programming interfaces (APIs). Mach extracts data from these APIs and uses it to ensure that Skube's Playlist and Search functions work.

Spotify's network API allows apps to extract data about artists, albums and songs directly from the Spotify catalog. The API also provides access to user data, such as playlists and music stored in its library.

The Skube project requires skills such as programming, chain building, wireless communications, data sharing with external devices, and building a case.

Remote-controlled lawnmower

Someone likes to mow the grass. Other people hate it. If you're one of the latter, why not solve the problem? If you're wondering how, check out this project.

The Lawnbot400 lawnmower will be a good test of your skills with mechanical and electronic devices.

The Lawnbot400 is a remotely operated lawnmower that consists of the following components:

A lawn mower with wheels and no control knob;

Two 12 B batteries to provide power voltage of 24 B;

A sturdy metal frame and a pallet for fixing lawnmower and battery mechanisms;

Two electric motors to move the mower

A transmitter and a remote control receiver that can be used to control the lawnmower.

Electronic components, including the Arduino fee.

The metal frame and wheels are the main

part of the project. Design requires good mechanics skills, not to mention the tools you need. There are no strict and strict rules - ingenuity will be your best friend.

Once the frame is ready, you will need to install electric motors. You can use any - those installed on the Lawnbot400 were taken from a wheelchair. Whatever electric motors you use, their position should be adjustable so you can adjust the tension of the drive chain. This will require a set plate.

The speed of the lawn mower is regulated by an electric motor controller specially designed for this purpose. It puts variable voltage on the electric motors. The controller itself is controlled by a signal of latitude-pulse modulation (SHIM) transmitted by the Arduino board. The electric motor controller converts the values of SHIM 0-5 B into a voltage of 0-24 B in the DC, which is fed to the electric motors.

The next step is to install a mower on the frame. Again, this will be a test of your mechanics and ingenuity skills.

The final stage of assembling this mechanical

structure is the installation of batteries. The weight of the batteries is high, so installing them behind the rear wheels will significantly improve control over the mechanism, as the batteries will act as a counterweight.

It's easy to manage a lawnmower. Move the left control lever upwards, and the left wheel will start moving forward. Move the right control lever backwards and the right wheel will move backwards. Move both levers forward, and the lawnmower will go forward. The Lawnbot400 can unfold with a radius of zero.

Security is a very important factor in working on this project.

The Lawnbot400 is a very unsafe mechanism. For this reason, it is very important that the frame and attachments of the mower are created to high quality standards.

At this stage there is an opportunity to improve Lawnbot400. For example, we could fully automate it by building a GPS system and sensors. It would also be possible to connect the electric motor to the leading shaft of the mower to automatically charge the batteries.

To ensure that the user does not lose the lawnmower, it is built into the fuse. It is another Arduino board that controls the power relay at 60 A. This fuse disables the power supplied to the electric motor controller if the signal sent from Arduino becomes very weak.

Finally, on the transmitter there is an emergency blocker that stops the power supply to the electric motors if the need arises.

Conclusion

So what is an Arduino?
Arduino is a designer's fantasy flight in which there is no finite, specific set of details, and there are no restrictions on the variety of what can be assembled. Everything is limited only by your imagination. You can automate any process of your life with the help of the Arduino board and your creativity. This is a new world, a killer hobby and a great gift for both a teenager and an adult. Thousands of

people in the world have already realized this. In this book, we wanted to make life easier for beginners.

I hope, that you really enjoyed reading my book.

Thanks for buying the book anyway!